TAKE THIS ORANGE

TAKE THIS ORANGE

POEMS AND BALLADS

by

John Pudney

LONDON
J. M. DENT & SONS LTD

First published 1971
© John Pudney, 1971

Made in Great Britain
at the
Aldine Press · Letchworth · Herts
for
J. M. DENT & SONS LTD
Aldine House · Bedford Street · London

ISBN 0 460 07836 4

CONTENTS

NOTE. Certain poems have appeared in the pages of the following journals: *Ambit, Contrasts, Enigma, Poet, Poetry & Music, Transatlantic Review, Tribune, Twentieth Century, Words Etcetera, Workshop.*

Storm

This tempestuous English night,
Reminder of battles.
Dreamed battles copper-gleaming
In the frightened sky with bugles
And the purple battalions
Herding clouds into the roaring black of the wind.

But you can't have the bugles back
And the flags are laid up
In the nave of some safe church.
Names written there on a plaque
Will tell you that battles were not like that.

Go look for your fantasies
In the mauve sonnet
Oozing from the face of a napalmed child
Or the canticle of the granny dangling in her hat
In blast-glazed silence
From a suburban tree in summer bud.

Those bugles that raked your blood . . .
Your innocence can't hear them,
Sends you into this tempestuous English night
Striding life-size to meet head-on the wonder
Of being alive
With all your frailty a whisper
Loud inside your head
In the still centre of the tempestuous sky.

If you side-step this wonder you will die
All the inches to morning
All the English mornings till death.

Sweet

So my eyes died
In the sweet morning
When Peter thanked his gun
Like a woman
Stroked it tenderly
At least as he thought the woman
Would like it after fun
Hadn't found that out though
Never did
That kid
Who bled to death
Like a child
Wild-eyed wondering
At the purple red
Bud flower bud flower
As he bled bud flower
To death
In less than half an hour
In the sweet morning

Sculpture

Shape I lie with,
Texture upon my tongue,
The far-flung echo of my eye
Against wonder
In furthest sky
And thunder of silence.

Space I enter
To flirt with deflection,
To sift the flecks from dirt.
From the rejection of dross
To find the acceptable tarnishes,
To gain the fringes of
Uncontained loss,
All the enormous horror
And joy of the span
Of sentient man.

Curve I scan.
Line I follow
To glimpse through a split nerve,
Dead pan,
The small
Stooped stature
Of the most tall.

Space I enter,
Shape I lie with,
Seeking no place
But the centre,
The undimensional grace.

Song for Eight Sopranos

Death is safer than life
Than loving
Than living
    The safety in numbers of death
And loving is larger than life
And living is born in love
Love the singular hazard
Safety is death
    O save me life O love
    The ultimate safety
Ultimate life is love
The singular hazard
    Death is safer than life
    The safety in numbers of death
Love the singular hazard
    O save me life O love.

The Gaiety of the Night

The gaiety of the night
The black dresses
All the women in the black dresses
Dancing
With the gaiety of the night

The wind bending them
The black wind
Bending the women
The blacker black
Dresses

And the women
Dancing back
Bending back the wind
Intending
The gaiety of it all
The night
Blacker black

The Fragment of Stained Glass

The glory of God

Was auburn
Hair
Against the white belly of the morning

Was yellow
For the flaxen Easter
Shouting in the hedgerow

Was the blue
Skin
Of the sky
But filtered
Through the see-all eye
Of original sin.

When you Quoted Dragons

You quoted dragons as a hazard
But I'm more scared of the hardware

Dragons can be wooed
With ice-cream or with riddles
With a show of force or with love

Hardware can be countered only
With logic or with wire cutters
Or of course with common sense

And me
I'm silly with riddles
Loaded with love
Can threaten
And push ice-cream
But fail in logic
Get pinched by wire cutters
And common sense left me
When you quoted dragons

The Yell of Spring

Plenty of eagles
Warrior men
And women strong as beds
So comes the yell of spring
To plunder

Say what is palpable
O my lily
Say what is
What the harsh answer is
What the losers
Sniffing your shrill scent
Use for words
Or do they
O my lily
Find corruption
In silence?

Soar and roar and whore
Do they in the fine hills
In the spring-swept light
Plundering the
Folds and fallows of the palpable
The dusky mellow
Calculated climates

So comes the yell of spring

Aspect of Love

The love of you
Is as positive as guns
As quick as dolphins
As subtle as light
Or night good with sleep

I cannot keep
Such images
Honey amber safe in jars
Just as I cannot keep
The air you breathe or
Love's money that we spend
Untouched like breath like stars

Yet at the end
I shall not be so destitute at death
For love of you

The Yellow End of the Dream

The yellow end of the dream
Where the light broke through
Into the wounded black surmises

You were waiting there
Patiently
In the forgiving sun

I envied you of course
As a part of my nature
That had stayed innocent
Whose dreams folded around
Beloved images and held them close

Then I found
We were talking the same language
That you had been dragged
Wounded through the black landscapes
And that innocence
At the yellow end of the dream was shared

The Ladders

Summer
Like a year of sleep
Runs through my fingers

The share of you I shall keep
Is not the languors
Of long days
Or brief nights' bright
Discoveries

It will be the ladders
That led
To the lofts
In the sleeping head

Complaint

If these are your fakes
Protect me from your genuine pieces.
I thought I was adroit
With the adverbs of emotion
But you have conned me cold:
So what I most despise
Increases
Its heart hold.

Garden Seat

The cat liked the place all summer
That long summer
Presiding there
Because it caught the sun so much

It was a happy
Contented to be a half-forgotten
Prickly with peeling paint flakes
Dodgy about taking weight at one end
Garden seat.

Garden seat
Shapely
With nineteenth-century flourishes
Of wrought iron
Capricious in balance
Creakingly treacherous for lovers
But the children knew it as an altar
The cat their priest
Yawning pink benedictions
For daisy-chain weddings

Personalizing garden furniture
Is not on
For children
For a sleepy cat
Or for happy people who prefer people

Even the screamer
Who said the dear little old thing
Could be done up
And tried
To buy it to put in a patio

The cat slept on and died
At the end of that long summer
We will all die
Having been happy there
Even the fly
Clinging to eternity on flaking paint
In October

> And the garden seat
> Undoubtedly
> Having no heart
> Will adorn a patio
> And look smart

Growing

When they tolled the bell for my mother
          She had been a churchgoer
          And people across meadows
          Would wonder
          Who is it this time
          Would usually guess who
I was proud
The bell for my mother
And then my innocence
Through the silver saliva bubbles of my sobs
Gained in stature inches
          The Protestant bells
          Still carried meaning
          In that place
          Buried now by a motorway
          And a township
          With frantic roots
I was that much taller
Measured on the grass
Sob-felled in a doomed meadow
Listening for the bell to stop
With innocence stretching
Like a boy's limbs
And waking body
Waking while they tolled the bell
For my mother
          The death of customs
          And of places
          The Protestant requiem
          Without music in the draughty nave
          Unlocked for the thin prayers
          And silly hymns on Sundays
          Form a frieze
          Upon a factory skyline

And the wondering voices
They were not innocent
Summer-tilted across meadows
Innocence grew in the ache
Stretch of knowing
In the sobs the silver life-white
Life-lively sight
Of dark death
When they tolled the bell for my mother

Nativity

The room need not be tidy
Evidence of work is acceptable,
Wood shavings,
Ink stains,
Boot mud.

Food and drink:
Tea cups of course,
The overhang of a loaf,
Saturday's beer bottles,
Stores
Worth one fifth of a week's wages.
Evidence of living is desirable.
The television a diamond
Bright with other worlds
Looks good
But is irrelevant.

Love not too obvious:
The bed tenderly made
But not with clean sheets,
Nappies washed and hung
Next to the seductive bra,
Six bought roses,
Pills behind the alarm clock.

Now the child that is to be born
Wants only to measure
How far death is away
From the room,
How near the living is to life,
And how measureless the love
That brings him from eternity.
The biology of the thing
He knows by heart.

Waterfront

At the street corner slanted by night rain
The moral issues of the lighted rooms
Get spent

Gentleness has the sound of a wind
With a whistled tune on it
Or of your silence
Thinking the tune

The river our unease
Tide rise
Tide top and ebb
Unease is
Tranquillity

Tranquillity is never still
Unease is ripples

The lighted rooms
Four square with principles
Are safe from wind and tide
Till the next bomb falls

The street corner
Dangerous with joy
Offers no shelter

What it was Really Like

I

You hear your childhood voices
And the mother prayers
A long way off
The erotic ecstasies
Of a driving seat
That was a marriage bed
A long way off

And the screams
And the broken sentences
That plead for death
A long way off

Then the skylark
Inside your head
Tricks you into soaring song
While very near
And nearer
Moves
This old sickness
Tiptoe
Closing the doors of all your rooms

II

Can you hear me at the back?
This might be the last word
Or a foretaste of what it was really like.

People in our time burn themselves alive
For principles,
Are also burnt alive by others
For principles.
The idealist and the baby
Cooking
Smell much the same.
Can you hear the smell at the back?

What it was really like,
The sick smell of the peeling crust of skin,
Young man's sacrifice or baby's original sin,
Go out of the window
Like last night's love
Or the rare shy eagles that prey on pity
Hunted only by sighs
That drown in frowning skies
And yearning
And the talking points with the words
Over-stretching
Snapping off into stylized trifles
Fetching
Back only this yearning
For what it was really like
This burning.
Do you hear it crackle at the back?

Flinching

Easy enough to
Sink through three storeys of bed-sitters
And meet a king for breakfast
At street level
Carving mushrooms of curved sleep
Opening the frosted bottles of memory
For a glazed picnic
Which the king says the queen fancies

It's that sort of summer
And the poppy fields beyond the railings
Sigh for encounters with strangers
And beyond again
Most afternoons
A watery wet aqueous lip-curve allows
The lured swimmer to drown
In a shallow shimmer of sea light.

Easy enough to tap the sky
And listen to the reverberations
Which usually cause
The frolicking horses to pause
Tossing wise manes

Birth is easy
In the velvet beds of the evenings
And the desire to kill
Effortlessly aids the rising moon
Exalting the queen's throat
As she beckons the knife
In the king's hand upward
Through the night
Through the three storeys of bed-sitters

Life begins with the innocence
Of knowing this
And at the birth of your child
Facing the thin moustache of the registrar
Without flinching.

From the High Window

For the waking eye
This morning has no past.
London below this window
Proffers the innocence of a sleeping hand.

> your hand with the crook'd finger
> the unintended beckoning
> but we can sigh and skip that
> or
> could be a murderer's hand
> or
> one that gave the sacrament

Look down over London
This wide-angle twentieth-century panoramic
Sort of look tourists pay well for,
St Paul's Tower Bridge Westminster
The Post Office Tower bland
Swaddled in that
Wordsworth the very houses seem asleep
That innocence
And pathos
Evoking a lump in the throat
For people who have tried
Built something
Communicated
Died.

> surburban birdsong
> reality
> do we skip that
> the dawn chorus funnelled in concrete
> with the look
> at London soft with sleep?

This morning has no past
Only this stretched moment
Reality printed on it,
Brittle,
To put a finger through.

Let the day wait
For a sacrament
For furnishing with what we care for,
That whispered *caritas*,
And the mythology we crave,
Live for,
Can only have by giving.

There is no ancestry
To this waiting day
With its sleep-soft city
Dreaming traditions and motives,
With its birdsong
The unregarded prelude
To the booked alarm calls.

Now we must surely accept
Finger-tip pressure as a final demand
And the placing of despair.
Accept happiness
Not in a resonant blaze
Of the sun rising
But in this morning
With no past.

Rumpus

This night they are moving harpsichords
About the sky
In anticipation—
Well obviously something is going to happen
And obviously this could be heavenly music.
After the noisy sunset,
And the afterglow a humming purple foreboding,
You'd hope for peace
The passeth-understanding fatigue
Of quarrellers
Of lovers
Of the old priest in the dirty surplice.
You'd hope: but your nerves
Twanging silently at the raw skin of anticipation
Wouldn't let you believe
Even his soiled benediction.

Such delicate instruments
Sensitive to climate.
The Italians covered their earlier ones in leather or velvet
Which still look pretty
Long after the tuning gauges are lost.
How can they make such a noise
Moving them
In a night sky especially
Which should be douce
Proliferating for music-lovers
In dark languors?

How does it come that they need several?
How many, in how many positions,
So many
Unwieldy cumbersome yet so delicate
In statement and retort

Or when engrossed
Proffering the potent modesty of the continuo
For some great sound
That drives us down through the floor of the night
And all our teeth drop out.

Will they never make up their minds
About the positions
Of these harpsichords in the sky
And stop the grating
Humping and putting down
The thumping scuffing across
The fringes of the nerves
The blocking of flights and exits
For the thoughts that want air?

Think then, where are our harpsichords
That we might leave
Cherished in prayer-soiled leather
Love-stained velvet
With the tuning gauges missing?
It's a notion
But only for the moment it takes them
To fidget a keyboard through two degrees.

Or what of the nightmare
We have here in a suave bottle
Well-notched
And just a little will thicken
The hair on the chest
And lower the price of Mary Magdalene?
Its dream-tots soften the shadows
Of hardening years
My round your round cheers

But do not soften the shock of their shifting
Their vacillations,
Or even fill a pause
Of this moving of the harpsichords
About the sky.

Dismiss the idea too
Of heavenly music.
We know a lot.
In the shop down our road
They sell the secrets of life
And in that factory on the cultural outskirts
They determine sexes.
We can live by programmed injection,
Can love safely in the sealed-off cubicles.
And the heavenly music
Is in our pipes,
Nippled for the new born
Automatic gear-change for the dying
And OK my dearest switch on
You're nearest.
This night they are moving harpsichords
About the sky
Not just for that.

All the space
This side of death
Seems to be needed
For this getting ready
This unrhythmical
Rumpus
With the delicate harpsichords
How many in how many positions
This side of death.

My Mornings Get Fewer

Kiss my eyes shut
So that I see the petals of the morning
Alight on the limpid river
And on the velvet moles of a wrist
In a single epic thought.

Do I throw this away too,
The nectarine flush
Behind my eyes,
And let you paint the morning
With circus colours
To amuse me?

My mornings get fewer
So perhaps I should forsake
The epic blaze in the sky
With prayer that moulds a wrist
Beyond the fringes of your radiance
And in the circus colours
Of compatibility in laughter
I should look for the clown,
Mankind upside down,
The frown compatible with
The laughing mouth.

Surround me with mirrors:
I will avoid the confrontation.
Guilt is easily come by:
A prison is soon built with bright words.
The aeroplanes of escape
Face the feasible runways
Waiting only for the sky to grin.

Any clown
Flushed with suffering
Thin with exultation
Wearing my temperament
Can go through the act and win,
Can believe in the feasible,
Break prisons,
Make faces at solemn mirrors,
Ride the escape routes,
Earning his pittance
Of petals in the limpid palm
Of the morning,
Knowing that mornings get fewer.

But the clown I have to find
Beyond the fringes of your radiance
Among the doubts that hang round windows
In the high-rising storeys
Of my mind
Knows how to count the loss of mornings.
When the sky grins
At the traditional postures
He shoulders the act
His burden packed
With the exultations with the frolics
With the sins
Of my times and my temperament.

Child of this Century

I am a child of this century
And grow old with it,
Older having learnt little,
Discovering much
Too late too soon.

Perhaps when the guarded firelight
In a safe nursery
Played upon the mellow-sick years
Of King Edward VII
And the horses were lovely
In the eye of a child of a foxhunter,
The devil was already in the harness room,
Shuffling his notices of sale,
Dismissal and doom:
And you loved him for what you couldn't see,
His tail.

When the painted horses went to war
It was a time of flags,
Their false innocence and heart-lift
And Albert King of the Belgians
The colour of embers, defiant,
King George V seen at Windsor
Stiff with good, smaller than our blacksmith,
Kaiser Wilhelm whiskered
Skewering somebody's baby,
The white distant Tsar
Beautiful as a playing card
Dealt on a crimson cloth.

Why were they crying
Among the oil lamps
And praying so much.

With God on the right side
With the jolly wounded-soldiers?
Crying when the devil would ride
On a motor bike
Accepting love with a nod
On his way to greet the dead?
So many by that November,
So noble,
And you loved him for what
You couldn't remember, Not
His goggles
But the horns on his head.

Then with the bonfires and the bell-ringing
And the soldiers turning into people,
The motor bike could have been forgotten
The flags mourned for,
The people trusted more than the soldiers,
Innocence recovered
In bright nights without love.
But it was love you were after.

There are the clocks
In the windy towers of my head.
How to keep pace with them
To listen to them in the night,
Heart-stopping for the next chime
Upon pillows of regret,
Sheets wet with sweat
Of slow guilt and a pendulum
Grazing the quilt?

But time:
This is clockwork
Or electrically driven
Processing hours
While the winds in the head's towers,

Wild from nowhere to nowhere,
Carry the laughter of cursory boys,
The hornpipes of doomed pilots,
The scent of the lily thighs
Of Anna in a spring meadow
With a view of the city
Shaped by attic windows.

The machinery serves purposes
Tells me the boys had pox
The dancers died badly
And there was no meadow
In that brown city
And of course spells out the time.
But this precision
Does not deny me Anna
Or her children or the laughter
Of poxy companions
Or their children
Or the antics of the doomed
And their lack
Of children.
It is just the mechanism
Ensuring
I don't have them back.

The onward drive
The drive home
Into the otherwhere of night
The night drive
Beneath the dangerous clouds
On familiar roads
With the known mileage
Yields associations
Landmarking the meaning of people
And their inferences

The impact of events
Their bruises and their poultices
Birthdays and estrangements
And some furtive deals
Done with mirrors.
These can't be forgotten
However often
The collect for the day or the engine oil
The terms of reference or even the make of car
Be changed.

When Christ thumbs a lift now
And says you know who I am
Good thing you stopped
He isn't here for the accident,
The beautiful one dying.
Doesn't he want to know how
Kids can die so squalidly?
Shall I try to say it,
Braking hard?
And the familiar traffic lane
Squeezes in,
Distorts
With the sick fright of headlights
Filling the brain's tunnels.

More likely the threat
From the passenger seat
Is the diffident knife
And the casually worded
Demand
For my money
And you can drop me
At the next corner
And I shouldn't try to follow me
If you want to keep out of trouble.

There is no safe way home
Through the familiar road signs
Or by good deeds
Or pious afterthoughts
Or the possession of a well-tuned engine.
In this over-insured century,
There is no way home
That isn't dangerous.

The Next Meal

Old women tell me this,
               and doctors
And sometimes solemn children
With sticky fingers on my surfaces
Tell me . . .

And I look aside,
Wiping stickiness and words
               and glances
Of appraisal from my nature,
Looking for truth
Between the mirror and the crucifix
Upon a wall
That is neither prison nor sanctuary
But a habit.

The last word will never be found
This side of the wall
Or beyond, in the sunny pavilions
And the fleet-footed slopes
Of giddy mountains
With motherly foliage.
The last word is eked out only
Of the solitude
Enforced at death.

So I look aside
In pride
At this mortality I find
Upon your breath, my breath,
Mingling, lingering,
With hints of truth
As a way of living,

A comparable achievement to having children,
Or a fight for principles
Knowing that the last word is there
Breathed at the final solitude.

But doctors,
Old women,
Sometimes solemn children
Talk despair.
Telling me this,
Telling . . .

Then it is that your kiss
(Remembered or
Better still immediate,
There)
Is sometimes like a whole season
Of grace, sometimes
Certainly the only reason
To look for the next meal.

The Astonishment

The astonishment came
With the cobbles
Through the feet
And was prolonged:
Came with a dark search for an inn
A century behind a façade
Of fuel pumps, fun machines.
      The feet ungainly.
      Shall I ever dance again?
      Or tiptoe in a bedroom?
That despondency was the slippery black wet
Spread over the small treachery of the cobbles.

And the astonishment, I say, like flutes
In a sunrise, possessing the whole body vertical,
With the feet on the cobbles,
And prolonged.

      I had thought astonishment till then
      Like meteorite
      Good or evil fizzing left or right,
      Or overnight blighted blossom hope dashed,
      Or the bright revelation
      Splashed on the wall of an end house,
      Some see-through sight
      Penetrating as disaster,
      Sudden.

But this went on,
The finding entering of the inn
As irrelevant as fuel pumps fun machines.

It continues with the rhythm
Of my body preposterously awake
With the territories of my mind
Ransacked for reasons.
It is a climate now
That deranges the placid run of the seasons.

Greenwich

The weather changes and the season,
Aspirations, frontiers change.
      They calculated and they laid down this meridian.
Time and change run over it
Measuring time and territory, known, unknown,
Its gentle rule stands fast.
      They calculated and they laid down this meridian.

See how
    the wedge of snow from the North Sea
    comes between the winter windows of heaven
    and St Paul's
The weather changes and the season
    spring from the south west
    blanches the cherry orchards of
    the fair polluted estuary
Aspirations, frontiers change
    summer-warmed, the artifacts
    of Wren, of Inigo Jones are cooled
    silvered by a harvest moon
    riding the smoke-stacked haze
    and the high-rising storeys,
    slotted with lives,
    looming larger than life are
    diamond-bedecked with an incandescent splendour
    of metered light

The weather changes and the season
  light captured by Canaletto, Turner,
  is never there again
  not quite yet always there
Aspirations, frontiers change
  men draft the margin of a motorway
  where Tallis, mean fellow, sweet songwriter
  lies in decent orderly dust.

The weather changes and the season,
Aspirations, frontiers change.
Time and change run over it,
The arbitrary line,
Innocent measure of goodwill, gentle, benign.
   They calculated and they laid down this meridian.

Take this Orange

Sometimes the wasted years assemble
Begging forgiveness
And I am less a god than an animal
Attending
With a psychiatrist's compunction
To their needs.
Then your head lilting
A stray hair with singular unruly force
Pleads
A line of cruelty
A god-like elbow of rejection.

For me there is this traffic in guilt
A fumbling with a tired currency.
I can rationalize too,
Taking this money
To dole out the medicines of remorse
Unblessed sacraments
From the test-tubes and retorts
Of analysts.
          And these are good people,
Objective as engineers when out of bed,
Their poultices wholesome
Their protocol as rigid as daffodils.
When they say yellow they mean yellow.
And I can say give me a leg-up into this cloud
So that I can scan the mysteries
And interpret and be a
More articulate animal.

But still you come into the corner of my eye
Taking your parallel stance,
Your indifference nudging my senses
Grudging the time I am taking
With administration.

II

When I offer you
The dead of two world wars,
The shake of your head,
Perceptible hair quiver,
Bids me smile
At the sepultures that adorn the events
And the crops that thrust up
Through paved-over mass graves.

From the corner of your mouth
Dangles the thought that
It was all too big.
Yes it was all too big.
And that bit about my heel slipping
Over the slippery stench
Of a rib cage?
        (Was it a man or a woman?)
That is to be a baroque sigh
Among furled flags.
Then the footnote
About how soon the dead smell dead.
And the postscript you must have been brave.
And Christ! Won't you listen?
Everybody was brave.
Everybody was good.

You admire the sunburn
On my arm and turn the palm.
Your cruelty is not the expected driven nail
But the swoop of a kiss
Swallow-light assertive calm.
Were the wasted years
The wars in my head
For this?

III

Fill the night with this orange I give you
It is real.
It is the loud bright banality of
Your unconcern.
Peel it thoughtfully
Destroying no illusions.
Let the skin drop indolently
To a ground level somewhere
Infinitely far,
Distant as war-dead, wasted years.
Some truth will come with the eating of the orange.

The years cannot be forgiven
You see them in the blood
Feeding the wrist
Of the hand that gave you the orange.
The wars exist
In the love I offer in exchange
For the parity of half an orange.
I am less an animal
I am the events, the delinquencies, the blemishes,
As you share the orange
With cruel fairness.

The orange has filled the night.

When I Wanted the Sunset

Over the slopes, my only way down,
Range the huge chairs and tables of reason
Set out to receive the bigger thoughts
That will assemble for the sunset.
And me, I shrink.

Even to have the fears of a high diver
Would be better,
At least to spring out and down
On a scream
And hit the sunset with a still-open mouth.

Better than this apprehension
With the skin drawing closer,
Panic clogging the feet,
And the blurring of the wounded blue
Of the eyes that seek the sunset.

Now stature, seeking, shrinks
With ridiculous gestures like a shot man.
A silly jig attempting dignity
Dodges this way and that, against time,
With putty footsteps
Patterning the huge inertia
Of chairs and tables.

Furniture
Set out for the impending
Reasonable thoughts
That will sip the sunset
And savour its ending
And swallow its hopes.

Before
I have time,
Before they draw
Night up over the slopes
Over their knees
And my only way down.

Night Piece

Your footfall on the steps of my white sleep
Has crossed the tender violence of our living,
The creases of the cast-off words
And dregs of thoughts in cups.

The time of honeysuckle also passes.

In the steep flights of my white sleep
Your footfall pauses:
And the breathing grasses bent
Seething somnolently thriving
Yield their scent.
Love is not honeysuckle
But a white event.

The time of honeysuckle also passes.

Innocence

Are you also the child
That untroubles my sleep,
Leaves wonderment
As first light recognizes
Thresholds behind my eyes
And kindles this day's love?

The child is
You and me, the shared
Presence that cleaves cold
Through the steam of dreams
Whose gesture strikes
The threatening tents of night.

Am I also the child
That can walk with you
On nights when London is ours
And we canvass the mysteries
And confront despair
With the touch of love
That fingers only air?

Antipodal Thought

The exuberant moment
Stilled
With the drip-wink of water
Off the poised oars
An overtone of measurement

While there was nothing to say
I thought of you in that other climate
Away
Laughing like sun on water
But upside down
With this moment this hour this day
A drip-wink reminder
Of exuberance
Obedient to Galileo
Yet laughing like sun on water
Like now
Defying the acknowledged geography

The Noah

The lonely look you noticed
Is not discrimination and not lack-love,
But just the parched screaming
Of a prophet
Who doesn't want to play Noah
And listen to the other people drowning,
Doesn't know how to save them,
Doesn't know how not to want to save them,
Or to save himself from being Noah.

Could be Simple

When it is simple,
When the stirring of your dreaming finger
Sends a scream through my bowels,
When I can think aloud
And you answer my thought by silence,

When I enter the temple of your ear
Without wearing words,
Or I walk through the suburbs of reason
Dressed in your smiles,
Or when a mirror misted with trifles
Laughs at us,
Then we achieve parity.

Then we are separate,
Say blades of grass
That rain may nourish or sun parch
And one or both could be stepped on,
Eaten by a cow or scythed
By a salesman demonstrating
An electronic cutter.
Like grass exuberantly in growth,
One and both, we thrive,
Acclaim that, care and matter.

Let me take the fear out of this;
Let us try
Accepting the lips upon the instep,
Compassion in the worshipping eye.
Then it is simple.

The Archaic Thunder

Should I offer you this Arctic meadow
For grazing our thoughts,
Even though
We wouldn't be out of reach
Of the archaic thunder?

Blood is not changed, I think
By shift of climate.
Only behaviour
Which lounged by the Equator,
Thinking the tinkle of ice in long drinks,
Appreciates the hard liquor
In the long twilight
Where violet and orange shadows
Fence-in grazing thoughts
On snow.

And the snow is also acquainted
With archaic thunder.

Instead
Let me offer you this afternoon tea
And notice the hole in your sock,
The comic intrusion of nakedness
At a time when we are stripped,
When we are nowhere much
And the archaic thunder
Doesn't frighten us much,
Is rather
Like love and death
That much
Part of the scene.

Mortality

When I taste upon your breath
Sunrise bursting like a grape,
Golden and green,
I lose track of the negatives
We made of ourselves:
But I don't lose my identity.

No, in that positive moment,
When I hear your quietness
Listening behind day's door,
Though the rehearsed dialogue
Dries on my tongue,
My lips printing me on you,
You on me,
Establish our two natures.

When the shy honeys of your life
Beneath your arm
Are stretched against the nostrils of my reason,
Your identity comes like an anthem
Into the gold-green morning.

And all the discipline
Of our mortality,
Both yours and mine,
Asserts its gender.

Love's structure is
Apparent, yes and strong,
Is visible
When the sun is up,
Marking our shadows separate,
Each intent
Upon its own mortality.

Absence

You have left too much in this empty room
At the time of sleep.
Your laughter hangs on the door
And your wisdom is folded over the chair
And your goodness is in the air
And I can't stop breathing can I?

You have left too much in my care,
Too much that we share.
You are sharing my prayers with me
But not my dreams.
And I can't stop sleeping can I?

You have left too much of my life
Which I wanted to give you:
You have left too much of your own.

I may be alone
But I can't stop living can I?

Night Narrative

The fact that God stopped the clocks
While we were trimming our unbeliefs
Shortened that night
But lengthened our lives.

That is if you measure lives
By what happens what is done
By the striking of silence
And of the half-spoken
Gleanings of the high harvests
That are under the eye of God.

So in the standstill
In this noon blazing in the night
When notions of God
Were put to the sickle
And we were looking at one another
A long way off
We were close in wonder
Under the eye of God.

And the thunder of this
Booming in the sallow hills of morning
Started the clocks.

Now

The white rope from the sky
Is not a portent
Is not the sound of time
Tuning the harps
Is not the scald of summer
Upon spring's lips.
It is the acceptable
Accepted
Now.

The white rope
Biting its calm
Stress
Into my nature
Is not for another day
Or for always
Or for never.

You are the white rope from the sky.

Acknowledgment

To travel
Further and further
Into the night with this image
(Its white radiance)
Is less a reward in itself
Than an affirmation
That the day was palpable
And that you were the white truth
In the radiance of the day.

To travel
This far alone
Is to acknowledge
That what was singular in me
Needed your singularity
To fire the chaste
Spare skelton of truth
Wearing its lustre
Further and further
Into the otherwhere of night.

October End

In the last morning of that October
In the erect morning
The ground mists horizontally folded
And the sun ruled
Over the innocence
Of a fulfilled summer,
Over the innocence
Of a harvested country,
Over the innocence
Of my granary of wonderment.
You were present
In the eye of the sun.

And the passing of that October
So genially
Toward my past,
The surrender in a golden light
Of that garnered country
Stripped to its innocence
Awaiting the handling of hard times
The ice-hold of the winter solstice,
Had the grace of good love.

Then the drift of leaves
Like burnished vessels
Into the air's compassionate
Limpid stillness
Was rehearsing an old music,
Exempt from youth and age,
Even from the indifferent
Sequence of seasons.